VOL. 2

Jesus

MILESTONES

Connecting God's Word to Life

LifeWay Press® Nashville, Tennessee

Student Ministry Publishing

Ben Trueblood
Director, Student Ministry

John Paul Basham
Manager, Student Ministry Publishing

Karen Daniel
Editorial Team Leader

Andy McLean
Content Editor

Stephanie Livengood
Production Editor

Amy Lyon
Graphic Designer

Requests for permission should be addressed in writing to LifeWay Press®, One LifeWay Plaza, Nashville, TN 37234.

ISBN: 978-1-5359-6584-2
Item Number: 005816979

Dewey Decimal Classification Number: 204
Subject Heading: RELIGION/ RELIGIOUS EXPERIENCE, LIFE, AND PRACTICE

Printed in the United States of America.

Student Ministry Publishing
LifeWay Resources
One LifeWay Plaza
Nashville, TN 37234

We believe that the Bible has God for its author; salvation for its end; and truth, without any mixture of error, for its matter and that all Scripture is totally true and trustworthy. To review LifeWay's doctrinal guideline, please visit www.lifeway.com/doctrinalguideline.

Table of
CONTENTS

Milestones was developed by the creators of *Bible Studies for Life: Students*, which exists to point students and student leaders to the application of biblical teaching to everyday life through weekly group Bible studies and additional resources. Every lesson within *Bible Studies for Life* contains a bible study that points students to Jesus, is rooted in Scripture, and provides application for living in today's context. The topics and subjects chosen in each quarter of *Bible Studies for Life* fit within a larger framework called *Levels of Biblical Learning*. *Levels of Biblical Learning* consists of ten theological topics we believe students should grasp before graduating high school. These include:

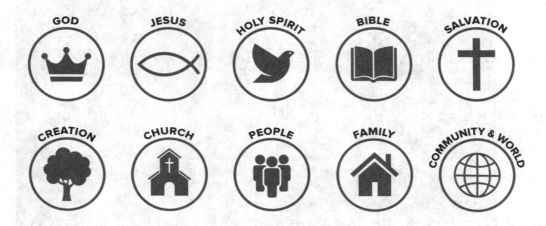

Within these ten topics are 52 theological statements, which make up the core content students would be exposed to and learn each year as they go through *Bible Studies for Life*. The quarterly topics and Scripture passages that make up each lesson in *Bible Studies for Life* are tied the framework of *Levels of Biblical Learning*, which guides the Scripture selection.

While we are able to connect students to the *Levels of Biblical Learning* and the theological statements in each lesson of *Bible Studies for Life*, we wanted to provide a resource capable of going deep into the weight and significance these levels have for personal faith and discipleship. This is what *Milestones* seeks to do. Over the course of six volumes, each of the 52 theological statements will be explored in depth, noting both the theological importance and personal application each has for everyday life. By going through these six volumes, we hope students will grow in their personal knowledge and understanding of God and His world. We also pray that God will use these resources to equip another generation to boldly proclaim the truth of the gospel in a world where Jesus—the truth—is desperately needed.

This Bible-study book includes eight weeks of content for group and personal study. Each session is divided into the following components:

ENGAGE

Each session opens with a *Levels of Biblical Learning Statement*, which gives an overview of the session's topic. Following the statement, each session contains an introduction to help your group as you begin your time together, setting up a natural transition into the material for each week.

DISCUSS

The Discuss section expands upon the *Levels of Biblical Learning Statement*. During this time, groups will explore Scripture, answer questions, and engage with additional content to help explain the session statement.

LIVE IT OUT

The Live It Out section is designed to close out your group time by calling out three specific points of application under the headings of Christ, Community, and Culture. By doing so, this section seeks to demonstrate specifically what the session material teaches us about Christ, how to live in Community, and how to engage with Culture.

DOING, BEING, AND APOLOGETIC STATEMENTS

This section also contains Doing, Being, and Apologetic statements. These statements are directly related to the *Levels of Biblical Learning Statement*, and provide opportunity for the group to expand on what these doctrinal truths communicate about us as individuals, how we are to live, and how we might engage culture apologetically.

DEVOTIONS

Three personal devotions are provided for each session to take students deeper into Scripture and to supplement the content introduced in the group study. With biblical teaching and introspective questions, these sections challenge students to grow in their understanding of God's Word and to respond in faith.

LEADER GUIDE

At the back of this book, you'll find a leader guide to help you prepare each week. This guide will help you gain a broad understanding of the content and learn ways to engage with students throughout your time together.

1

THE PERSON OF CHRIST

LEVELS OF BIBLICAL LEARNING STATEMENT

Jesus is fully God and fully man, and despite being tempted while on earth, remained altogether free from sin.

Jesus is not like anyone else who ever lived. No religious tradition has anyone like Him. Nobody even comes close. Some religions have people who claim to be hearing directly from God. Others believe God is in the trees or in the sun. But Jesus is something completely different and, at least on the surface, a little strange: He is fully God and fully human. He's both. All at the same time.

Why is it important that Jesus is both fully God and fully man?

THE WORD

It's difficult to imagine something that is two separate things at once. Try to think about a perfectly round edge that is also totally jagged. Or a snail that is also a falcon. We're not good at thinking like this, because it is what we call a contradiction.

Try to imagine more contradictions like this. What other things can only be one thing or the other—not both?

Even more difficult to imagine that happens to also be a central idea in Christianity: Jesus was totally, completely, perfectly human. But He was also totally, completely, perfectly God. How could this be?

What are some things you know to be true about humans?

What are some things you know to be true about God?

Read Genesis 1:1-3.

Investigate the text. What does verse 1 tell us about God and what He did?

Who else was around when God was doing this (v. 2)?

These three verses—the first three verses of the Bible—are the first place we see what people call the Godhead, or the Trinity. It tells us something about God and what He's like: He's one God, one Divine Creator. But He also exists as three distinct Persons. We see the first Person of God in verse 1. He's the One who created everything. We see the second Person of God in verse 2. God's Spirit is never far from God, because they work, observe, and move together.

But verse 3 tells us something incredibly important. When God created everything, He did it by speaking. He used His Word. God, His Spirit, and His Word are three distinct Persons of the same Creator. We're going to focus on that third person: God's Word.

GOD'S WORD MADE FLESH

Our words have incredible power. They have the power to hurt, as well as the power to heal. However, God's Word is even more powerful: His Word created everything around you. God's Word came to prophets and kings, to shepherds and priests. Finally, God's Word did something incredible: it came in the form of a person.

> *In the beginning was the Word, and the Word was with God, and the Word was God. He was with God in the beginning. All things were created through him, and apart from him not one thing was created that has been created. In him was life, and that life was the light of men. That light shines in the darkness, and yet the darkness did not overcome it. ... The Word became flesh and dwelt among us. We observed his glory, the glory as the one and only Son from the Father, full of grace and truth.*
> **JOHN 1:1-5,14**

What amazing things do these verses say about the Word of God?

John went on to explain that when the Word became flesh, the world got to know Him as Jesus. To call this occurrence anything less than a miracle would be doing a disservice. Jesus was both fully God (because He is the Word-made flesh) and fully man (because He was born to a human woman), but there's something else about Him that is simply incredible.

> *Therefore, since we have a great high priest who has passed through the heavens—Jesus the Son of God—let us hold fast to our confession. For we do not have a high priest who is unable to sympathize with our weaknesses, but one who has been tempted in every way as we are, yet without sin.*
> **HEBREWS 4:14-15**

If Jesus were just a man, then He wouldn't be God. If He were only divine, it wouldn't be a big deal that He didn't sin. The fact is that He is both. And He was certainly tempted to sin.

Sin entered the world the second mankind put themselves above God. God told them not to do something, but they decided they wanted to be on the throne of their own hearts instead of God. But unlike human beings, Jesus overcame temptation—every single time. We have three examples of this for us in Scripture (Matt. 4:1-4). Jesus had the power to do anything He wanted. Instead, He was submitting Himself to God's timing, not waiting for "permission" from the devil.

When is it difficult for you to trust God's timing?

LIVE ON THE WORD

If God is the one in charge of the way we live, His Word is sufficient for us to rely on when the temptation to do otherwise comes along.

Notice what Jesus did here. He is the Word of God in the flesh, but He still used resources that we have available to us to show us how we can act like He does. His entire life was completely rooted in the Word of God—to the point that even when He was tired, hungry, and weak, it was the first thing out of His mouth.

Do you think that it is reasonable to expect humans to behave exactly like Christ did? Why or why not?

What do you think is something we can do to help us start to respond to temptation the way Jesus did?

Jesus' comparison of God's Word to bread was on purpose. Just like physical bread fills our physical needs and gives us physical strength, God's Word fills our spiritual needs and gives us spiritual strength—the kind of strength it takes to stand up to temptation. If we're going to be like Jesus and stand up to temptation, we need to follow His example and lean on the Word of God.

How many times did you eat yesterday? Would any of those meals have kept you from being hungry the next day? Why or why not?

How many times did you read God's Word last week? Were any of these "spiritual meals" enough to satisfy you for the next day? Why or why not?

Let's take a cue from Jesus, and commit ourselves to knowing and trusting God's Word like Jesus did.

LIVE IT OUT

BEING // Because Jesus took our sin and gave us His righteousness in its place we are now accepted into God's presence—even though we were once separated from God.

DOING // Because Christianity necessarily involves following Christ, we should continually live in obedience to His commands as an expression of our faith in and love for Him.

APOLOGETIC // Whereas many claim that Jesus was a good man or a great teacher, the truth is that Jesus is God (John 1:1,14; 8:58; 10:30).

CHRIST

Most ancient Jews would have put us to shame when it comes to knowing the Word of God, but Jesus is a cut above the rest. He lived and breathed nothing but God's Word: teaching it at every opportunity and letting it guide His actions, motivations, and desires. While His standard is one we will never reach this side of heaven, writing the Word on your heart is something you can begin doing right now (Prov. 7:3).

Can you quote a verse from memory? If so, write it out.

Commit to memorizing at least one verse this week. You may even start with one Jesus quoted. The first verse He would have memorized as a child is Deuteronomy 6:4-5: "'Listen, Israel: The LORD our God, the LORD is one. Love the LORD your God with all your heart, with all your soul, and with all your strength.'" Write out the verse you plan to memorize this week.

COMMUNITY

Even Jesus, the Son of God, didn't do everything by Himself. The majority of His ministry was spent investing in His closest friends. You probably have a godly community around you, too—at your church, perhaps in your family, and maybe in your friend group. Develop close godly relationships with the people around you and help each other through both the good and the bad times. Sometimes, it's the people around us who can give us the extra push we need to avoid temptation.

How do you think having godly people around you can help you avoid temptation?

CULTURE

In Ephesians 2, Paul divided people up into two categories: Those who are "dead in [their] trespasses and sins" (v. 1) and those who have been made "alive with Christ" (v. 5). Nothing has changed in the two thousand years since he wrote those words. The people around us are still divided up into those two categories. As followers of Jesus, we have a prime opportunity to demonstrate an alternative to living a life dead to sin and temptation.

Out loud, read Ephesians 2:1-5. What do you think the difference is between those who are "dead" and those who are "alive"?

What kind of life do you think would catch the eye of someone who doesn't know Jesus and make them ask, "I wonder what they have that I don't"?

Session 1

DEVOTIONS

I AM THE BREAD OF LIFE

In the Book of Exodus, when God introduced Himself to Moses, it was the first time in centuries God gave mankind a name by which we might know Him. To Moses, God referred to himself as "I AM" (Ex. 3:14).

The Gospel of John records seven "I am" statements spoken by Jesus; identifying Himself with the same "I am" of the Old Testament. He is the God who was, the God who is (meaning that He exists now), and the God who is coming back. Take a look at the way Jesus continued this beautiful practice of identifying Himself with elements of the Old Testament.

> "'I am the bread of life,' Jesus told them. 'No one who comes to me will ever be hungry, and no one who believes in me will ever be thirsty again.'"
> **JOHN 6:35**

Consider the grammatical tense of the words "I am." Any adjective added to those two words would give a descriptor that falls short of who God is. Any statement of God speaking only of the past, as in "he was," without affirming His consistency today suggests that God has changed. He has not. Any statement of God suggesting "he will be" presupposes that He is not already that way now. He is. Thus, God is the great "I am."

Thinking of the bread God gave the Israelites from heaven in Exodus, describe ways in which Jesus is similar.

Since Jesus is obviously not describing Himself as literal bread, what was He saying?

I AM THE LIGHT OF THE WORLD

Do not let the darkness of this world overwhelm you. If you are a Christian, you serve the God who overwhelms the darkness. Your Savior is the One who first said, "Let there be light" (Gen. 1:3) and it was so. So, do not let your heart be troubled by the darkness in your personal life, or in the world at large. Fix your hope in heaven where the light lives forever. The Bible talks about Jesus, the light, this way:

> Jesus spoke to them again: "I am the light of the world. Anyone who follows me will never walk in the darkness but will have the light of life."
> **JOHN 8:12**

As a Christian, you have something. You know the Light. Jesus is the Light of the world who shines in the darkness and the darkness has not overcome Him (John 1:5). He is simply greater. God is aware of the darkness. He knows about your pain. This is why Jesus' statement is significant and necessary. We all know the darkness well, but how many people in your life are acquainted with Jesus, the Light?

Exactly what is darkness? In what seasons of your life have you walked in it?

Journal a prayer inviting Jesus to light up the darkness in your life. Be specific and ask God to strengthen your trust in Him.

I AM THE GATE

The next two "I am" statements of Jesus revolve around the same metaphor of a sheep pen. The people of God are the sheep and Jesus is our Shepherd. The pen itself may be interpreted as a symbol of our sinful state. Other voices may call out to us as God's sheep, but we know His voice because He has given us His Holy Spirit and has spoken to us through His Word. Here we find ourselves penned in by our sin and no more capable of making a way out than a sheep has a way of making an escape from a stone pen. Jesus claims to be both the shepherd and the gate.

> *Jesus said again, "Truly I tell you, I am the gate for the sheep. All who came before me are thieves and robbers, but the sheep didn't listen to them. I am the gate. If anyone enters by me, he will be saved and will come in and go out and find pasture. A thief comes only to steal and kill and destroy. I have come so that they may have life and have it in abundance.*
> **JOHN 10:7-10**

This means He not only made the way for salvation, but He has also called us to it. Others had claimed to be the Messiah before Jesus came and many have had the audacity to repeat the claim since Jesus' life. Religious leaders of the years before Jesus' birth had weighed down God's people of Israel with man-made legal burdens impossible to carry. These impostors are like the sheep thieves and robbers in Jesus' metaphor. Instead of acting like a sheep thief who leads the sheep of God's people through some impossible way, Jesus is our Gate.

In light of this passage, why does God not allow His people to worship other gods?

Describe some of the "thieves" and "robbers" in your own life who would claim that there are other ways to God.

2

THE PERFECTION OF CHRIST

ENGAGE

LEVELS OF BIBLICAL LEARNING STATEMENT

Jesus was conceived by the Holy Spirit and born of a virgin, which means He didn't inherit the sinful nature passed down from Adam, which made Him fit to be our Savior.

Every person on earth shares something in common with every other person on earth: They have two parents. Now, not everybody knows both, or either of them, but that doesn't mean they don't have them. It's one of the simplest facts about human life: It takes two people to make a new person.

The same cannot be said of Jesus. His is the only case in history where a baby was born without an earthly father involved at all. And the implications for us today are huge.

Do you think it's easy or difficult for you to believe Jesus was born to just one parent?

SIN NATURE

Let's say you really have to sneeze, but for whatever reason you just can't. And it's driving you crazy. Some people have it a lot easier than others when faced with this annoying situation: They can look at a bright light and almost instantly begin sneezing.

Here's the crazy part: There's a name for this ability. It's called Autosomal Dominant Compelling Helioopthalmic Outburst Syndrome—or more simply (and more appropriately), ACHOO Syndrome. This is actually a trait passed down from your parents! If one of your parents has this syndrome, you have a 50 percent chance of having it, too.[1]

What is something—a trait, a quirk, a habit, a feature—you have that your parents also have?

Everything that makes us up comes from our parents. Their genes combined together to make the unique blend of DNA that made you. This is how God created us to be!

They've also passed something down handed to them by their parents, who got it from their parents, who got it from their parents, and so on, back to the beginning of time: a sin nature. We're born with hearts that love to sin. Nobody has to teach us to love it.

Sin has been a part of human nature since Adam and Eve sinned in the Garden of Eden. They were created to live in perfect community with God, but after they disobeyed God's command, they let sin corrupt their relationship with Him.

Read Genesis 3:1-7,20-24.

Last week we talked about how anything that sits in God's place on the throne of your life is sin, whether it's something "big" or something "small."

What do you think made Adam and Eve's actions sinful?

Why do you think Adam and Eve were kicked out of the garden? Why would it have been bad for them to stay there?

SINFUL HEARTS

Adam and Eve's disobedience upset the way humans and God would interact from that moment on. Before, they were able to walk and talk with God in paradise, but when they disobeyed Him, nobody was allowed back into the garden. Because they became sinful, their children would be like them: humans formed in the Image of God, but tainted by sin.

Take a look at what Paul had to say about the way sin affects all of us.

> And you were dead in your trespasses and sins in which you previously lived according to the ways of this world, according to the ruler of the power of the air, the spirit now working in the disobedient. We too all previously lived among them in our fleshly desires, carrying out the inclinations of our flesh and thoughts, and we were by nature children under wrath as the others were also.
> **EPHESIANS 2:1-3.**

How did Paul describe "this world" (vv. 2-3)?

How do "the ways of this world" oppose the ways of God?

Think about how Paul described the ways of the world in this passage. Those who follow it are disobedient. They are slaves to their fleshly desires. He calls them "children of wrath." He even said before coming to Christ, we were dead!

What do you think Paul meant when he compared those living in sin to people who are dead?

What does it mean to follow fleshly desires?

Paul's description sounds a lot like Jeremiah's words: "The heart is more deceitful than anything else, and incurable" (17:9). That word "incurable" means terminally ill. It's sick without any hope of getting better on its own. There's not a thing we can do to revive our dead, stony hearts. But that's not the end of the story. Not by a long shot.

JESUS RESCUES

Take a look at the marvelous gift Paul mentioned in the Book of Ephesians.

But God, who is rich in mercy, because of his great love that he had for us, made us alive with Christ even though we were dead in trespasses. You are saved by grace!
EPHESIANS 2:4-5

Let's see if we can understand two important words Paul used in this passage: mercy and grace. These words are similar, but have different meanings. If you're shown mercy, you deserve punishment but are spared from it. If you're shown grace, you get a free gift that you don't deserve at all.

When have you been shown mercy—you didn't receive a punishment you deserved?

When have you gotten something for free that you didn't deserve?

When God gave us Jesus, He was showing us mercy and grace at the same time. Even though we were born dead, with hearts that hate putting God on His throne, God loved us so much He made a way for us to be with Him, even though we don't deserve it at all.

Read Luke 1:26-35. What characteristics about Mary do you think made her the kind of person God would use to bring His son into the world?

Jesus is unique among the rest of the humans on Earth. For starters, He doesn't have an earthly Father. Jesus inherited everything that made Him human from His mother, while also avoiding the sin nature. He was tempted to sin, yes, but He never did. Paul said it this way: "He made the one who did not know sin to be sin for us, so that in him we might become the righteousness of God" (2 Cor. 5:21).

Like a lifeguard who rescues people from drowning, Jesus stepped in and rescued us from our sin.

Because of Adam and Eve, humans have been born into sin for all of history. But Jesus didn't inherit the same sin nature we did. He was the only One in all of history who was able to do what we couldn't do ourselves: save us from our sin and make a way for us to live in the presence of God.

LIVE IT OUT

> **BEING //** Because Jesus took our sin and gave us His righteousness in its place we are now accepted into God's presence—even though we were once separated from God.
>
> **DOING //** Because Christianity necessarily involves following Christ, we should continually live in obedience to His commands as an expression of our faith in and love for Him.
>
> **APOLOGETIC //** Whereas many claim that Jesus was a good man or a great teacher, the truth is that Jesus is God (John 1:1,14; 8:58; 10:30).

CHRIST

We have a big problem on our hands with this whole sin nature thing. We have nothing we can do to fix it ourselves, no magic cure to the condition we were born into. This is why it's so important Jesus came to save us, and why it is so important that He is who He said He is. Believing in Jesus is the first step to living a life empowered by His Spirit to accomplish the work that God has for us. And it's the only thing we can do to be saved from the penalty of death that comes from our rebellious hearts.

Describe the time you first met Jesus.

How did Jesus change you?

COMMUNITY

What comes to mind when you think of unity? You might think of a laboratory full of scientists each working small pieces of a really big problem. You may even think of a peaceful demonstration with people from all sorts of backgrounds holding signs in protest of something. It turns out both of these have something to do with what unity is: You are a unified group of people if you share a common goal.

The church today has the strongest thing possible to be unified around: Jesus Christ. When we believe Jesus is who He said He is and devote ourselves to knowing Him better, we become more like Him and carry out His work in the world around us. As we do this, we have brothers and sisters walking alongside us and affirming our faith, no matter how different we look or how much distance stands between us.

Why do you think it's important to be unified with other Christians?

What are the important things Christians need to agree on?

CULTURE

Some critics like to point out that the story of Jesus' virgin birth was something Jews copied from pagan myths and that Mary had Jesus the same way anybody has a baby. Unfortunately for them, the case for Jews making up the virgin birth just doesn't hold much water. The Jewish culture paid zero attention to the false beliefs of ancient Greece—after all, they had finally learned their lesson in captivity about giving allegiance to beliefs found outside of God's revelation in Scripture. They were surely eager to not repeat those mistakes. Statements like this are people's attempts to make something miraculous into something ordinary so they won't be held responsible for what it means if it's true.

Why do you think it is important to believe Jesus was actually born of a virgin?

Why do you think people are so quick to deny this fact?

DEVOTIONS

I AM THE GOOD SHEPHERD

After describing Himself as the gate in the previous verses, Jesus described Himself another way.

> *"'I am the good shepherd. The good shepherd lays down his life for the sheep.' ...*
> *'I am the good shepherd. I know my own, and my own know me, just as the Father*
> *knows me, and I know the Father. I lay down my life for the sheep.'"*
> **JOHN 10:11,14-15**

For context, sheep were tremendously important to their owner. Hired workers may have performed a decent job looking after the sheep, but would surely run for their lives when the wolves came. However, a truly good shepherd would risk his own life to save the lives of the sheep.

When God first made the "I AM" (Ex. 3:14) statement to Moses in the Old Testament, Moses was looking after sheep. Later, when David wrote many of the famous Psalms we know today, he was a shepherd looking after sheep (1 Sam. 17:34-36). Jesus fulfills in this text what countless Old Testament passages foreshadowed. Moses was a pretty good shepherd, but he ultimately had his shortcomings. David was a fiercely protective shepherd who came to be a good king, but he also had his failings. At last the truly Good Shepherd has arrived. His name is Jesus.

Describe Jesus' heart for the people of Israel as they were weighed down by burdensome laws God never wrote.

Describe what it is like to hear your Shepherd's voice.

I AM THE RESURRECTION AND THE LIFE

The sisters Mary and Martha have come to symbolize two approaches to Christ and life. Mary, based on her conduct in Luke 10:38-42, has come to personify the sweet, loving, affectionate kind of Christian who just wants to sit at Jesus' feet. Martha, with her business focusing on the household chores instead of just being with Jesus, has come to personify a distracted kind of Christian. We are told, "be like Mary, not like Martha."

Let's take a closer look at a different encounter Jesus had with these sisters. In this passage, we should strive to imitate Martha instead of Mary. Mary and Martha's brother Lazarus died. Mary, quite understandably, just felt intense pain and even spoke harshly to Jesus when He arrived deliberately late. Martha, trusting completely in Jesus despite her circumstances, showed remarkable faith.

"'Your brother will rise again,' Jesus told her. Martha said to him, 'I know that he will rise again in the resurrection at the last day.' Jesus said to her, 'I am the resurrection and the life. The one who believes in me, even if he dies, will live. Everyone who lives and believes in me will never die. Do you believe this?'"
JOHN 11:23-26

Thankfully, Jesus last statement in this passage also applies to believers today.

What should change in your view of death in light of the fact that Jesus is the resurrection and the life?

How should Christians grieve differently from those who do not know Christ?

I AM THE WAY, THE TRUTH, AND THE LIFE

The ancient account of the great "I AM" (Ex. 3:14) had come to life and was walking among us. The sixth of Jesus' seven "I am" statements appeared in a set of three.

> *Jesus told him, "I am the way, the truth, and the life. No one comes to the Father except through me. If you know me, you will also know my Father. From now on you do know him and have seen him."*
> **JOHN 14:6-7**

Jesus is the way. He is the way we may go to the Father, our Creator. He is the truth. Truth is innately exclusive. Anything contrary to the truth is a lie. Here, the truth itself is personified in Jesus. Jesus is the Life. This means anything we chase in this world outside of Jesus ends ultimately in death. There is no life apart from Jesus.

Strive, fight, excel, and grind. Still, you will not find life apart from Him.

Who was speaking in these verses? Who, then bears the weight of this truth?

Think about sharing the gospel of Jesus Christ with someone who sincerely holds to another religious worldview. How does this passage prepare your heart for these kinds of encounters?

3

THE MISSION OF CHRIST

ENGAGE

LEVELS OF BIBLICAL LEARNING STATEMENT
Jesus lived for the glory of the Father and taught that we should do the same through lives of worship, service, and sacrifice.

Why are we here? People have been trying to answer this question for centuries, for milennia, maybe even since the beginning of time. Philosophers debate about it and religions fight about it. Some people ignore the question and bury themselves in their work to try not to think about it. Some people throw up their hands in frustration and say it can't be known, so everything must be meaningless.

But Jesus knew exactly why He was here. And by seeing why He was here, we learn why we're here too.

If someone asked you why you think we're here, what would you say?

GLORIFY GOD

Have you ever tried to grow a plant? Some plants are extremely easy to grow: they do well in direct sunlight and shade and can still grow well even if you don't water them consistently. Others, like the Ghost Orchid, are pretty difficult. If you want to grow a Ghost Orchid, you have to make sure that they are attached to a bark mount with a specific glue and not moved around. Their environment should alternate between humid and dry and should be bright and sunny. Some people even use fans to keep the plants cool enough during the summer.[1] Talk about a needy plant!

A well cultivated garden with impressive variety and obvious care is beautiful to see, but it points back to someone important: the one tasked with keeping it. A gardener's garden reflects the gardener's talent.

> "I am the true vine, and my Father is the gardener. Every branch in me that does not produce fruit he removes, and he prunes every branch that produces fruit so that it will produce more fruit. You are already clean because of the word I have spoken to you."
> **JOHN 15:1-3**

Jesus called God a gardener. Calling God a gardener is not much of a stretch—after all, He's the ultimate gardener, not just of plants and flowers, but of the Universe. He made everything from stars and supernovas to ants and atoms!

What do you think God's ultimate goal was when He created everything?

> I will say to the north, 'Give them up!' and to the south, 'Do not hold them back!' Bring my sons from far away, and my daughters from the ends of the earth— everyone who bears my name and is created for my glory. I have formed them; indeed, I have made them."
> **ISAIAH 43:6-7.**

How does God's creation display His glory?

When Jesus came to earth, He had the exact same thing on His mind: the glorification of the Father. In fact, it was so heavy on His mind that the thing He talked about more than anything else—more than salvation, more than sin, more than injustice—was the kingdom of God.

WORSHIP GOD

In your own words, what is worship? How have you experienced worship before?

Worship is not just the second half of "praise." It isn't just the thing we do in church before the preacher preaches. Worship is the way you live your life. Paul gave some specific instruction to the Roman church about worship that help us see clearer what it looks like.

Therefore, brothers and sisters, in view of the mercies of God, I urge you to present your bodies as a living sacrifice, holy and pleasing to God; this is your true worship. Do not be conformed to this age, but be transformed by the renewing of your mind, so that you may discern what is the good, pleasing, and perfect will of God.
ROMANS 12:1-2

What did Paul mean by being a "living sacrifice?"

How did Paul connect our living to our worship in these verses?

When someone shows you mercy, they don't give you a punishment you actually deserve. Think of mercy this way. You got a speeding ticket. But when you showed up to pay it, the judge told you that you were no longer on the hook for it, even though it was your fault to begin with.

God showed us mercy by withholding the punishment for sin and giving it to Jesus, who paid the price in our place. This mercy is what Paul said should motivate us to "present [our] bodies as a living sacrifice." We tell God, "You bought and paid for me, so I am yours. Use me how you'd like me to be used."

What would it look like today for someone to tell God, "I'm yours. Put me to work"?

Just like we can tell what kind of tree we're looking at by seeing the kinds of leaves and fruit it produces, we can tell what kind of heart someone has by the things they do. If someone has a heart that is selfish and hard, they're not going to behave like someone whose heart is overjoyed to have been bought and paid for by Jesus.

LIVE HUMBLY

Knowing what Jesus has done for us is the first step toward accepting the gift He offers. He made Himself like one of us, suffered at our hands, and still cleansed us so we can enter into fellowship with God.

When Jesus washed the disciples' feet just days before His crucifixion, He told them they were supposed to take His example of humility and live it out with others.

In your own words, what is humility?

Have you ever encountered someone who was truly humble? What was it like to be around that person?

In his book, *The Purpose-Driven Life*, Rick Warren wrote that "humility is not thinking less of yourself; it is thinking of yourself less."[2] Some believe being humble means thinking you're less awesome than you are, but that isn't necessarily the truth. More accurately, the person who is humble thinks of themselves less often than they think of others.

Jesus is the prime example of humility. He had every reason to think highly of Himself: He was the sinless, eternal Son of God! But instead of bragging about who He was, He lived entirely for the glory of the Father. And the life Jesus is one we can model ours after—full of worship, service, and sacrifice.

Do your actions prove that you've been purchased by Jesus' blood? Why or why not?

Are there things you feel the Holy Spirit prompting you to change?

LIVE IT OUT

BEING // Because Jesus took our sin and gave us His righteousness in its place we are now accepted into God's presence—even though we were once separated from God.

DOING // Because Christianity necessarily involves following Christ, we should continually live in obedience to His commands as an expression of our faith in and love for Him.

APOLOGETIC // Whereas many claim that Jesus was a good man or a great teacher, the truth is that Jesus is God (John 1:1,14; 8:58; 10:30).

CHRIST

Have you thought about how incredible it is that Jesus had every opportunity to become the richest, most powerful person on the planet, but instead spent His time with twelve individuals who often just didn't get it? He did this because He was in no way looking for glory for Himself. He wanted everything He did to bring glory to the Father.

Most of us probably won't ever have the opportunity to become the richest, most powerful person on the planet, but we absolutely do have the opportunity to glorify God through our lives.

What does a life that brings God glory look like?

Be honest with yourself: What or who does your life glorify?

COMMUNITY

On our own, we're pretty good at forgetting what we're supposed to do. We might get caught up in momentary visions of grandeur or in seeking the approval of someone who doesn't ultimately matter. Fortunately for us, God built in an accountability system of other like-minded believers. We can do our part to help the people around us remember what it is they're here to do, which is to bring God glory at every turn rather than seeking glory for themselves.

What are ways that we can encourage each other to glorify God in our everyday lives?

CULTURE

Glorifying God isn't something we're supposed to do in the quiet of our own homes or on our own apart from the rest of the world. Instead, we should be the ones on the forefront of great things. We should be excellent musicians and artists, athletes and thinkers, and friends. But we shouldn't do it so that we can get recognition and glory for ourselves. We live this way so that, through us, people see only the One we're glorifying: Jesus Christ.

Why do you think living a life that glorifies God means we should be excellent at everything we do?

How can living with excellence help point others to God?

DEVOTIONS

I AM THE VINE

Jesus' final "I am" statement in the Gospel of John comes in John 15:4 and 5.

Remain in me, and I in you. Just as a branch is unable to produce fruit by itself unless it remains on the vine, neither can you unless you remain in me. I am the vine; you are the branches. The one who remains in me and I in him produces much fruit, because you can do nothing without me.
JOHN 15:4-5

We are absolutely, completely dependent on Jesus. On our own, we are not "good," although the world may try to tell us otherwise. The voice that says self-esteem is spiritual sinlessness comes from the enemy. Jesus is the vine from whom we know the way, see the truth, and have eternal life. If we mere branches are separated from the Vine, we are then left to our own sinful devices whose ultimate fruit is hell.

Examine your heart carefully. Do you ever find yourself thinking you are a good person and don't need Jesus' help?

Surely Jesus' use of the word "remain" is strategic. What did He intend by that particular word?

Be honest: Have you attempted to connect to the Vine only when you feel like you need Him?

I HAVE COME THAT THEY MAY HAVE LIFE

When we studied the third of the "I am" statements, we saw Jesus make another statement. The "I am" statements tell us about who Jesus is. He is one with the Father who introduced Himself to Moses through the burning bush. Now, why did He come to us?

Describing the false voices that would lead God's people astray, Jesus said:

> A *thief comes only to steal and kill and destroy. I have come so that they may have life and have it in abundance.*
> **JOHN 10:10**

Jesus came so that we may have life. Let that statement realign your heart if you hold any resentment toward God, if you misunderstood just how intimately personal He is, or if you thought the gospel of Jesus Christ had little to do with how you live.

However, as you take the step of belief in Jesus' mission to give us life, do not neglect to take the next step of belief: fully grasping that we should have this life in abundance. He did not come that we would have a small and empty type of life. He has come for us to have life that abounds, overflows, erupts, and envelops others who are now in the darkness that once grasped us.

Given the cost of the gospel and the sacrifice of Jesus on the cross, have you been living out a life worthy of the gospel?

How do you imagine it makes God feel when we live as though we were dead in sin?

WATER TO WINE

Jesus came for us to have life and have it in abundance. That abundance is exquisitely depicted in the ceremonial water vats Jesus used to perform His first miracle.

> *"Fill the jars with water," Jesus told them. So they filled them to the brim. Then he said to them, "Now draw some out and take it to the headwaiter." And they did.*
> **JOHN 2:7-8**

The miracle would have been just as astounding if Jesus performed it with only a single communion cup, but He filled entire ceremonial vats.

> *Jesus did this, the first of his signs, in Cana of Galilee. He revealed his glory, and his disciples believed in him.*
> **JOHN 2:11**

This was His first miracle, but the grand finale of His miracles will take place in the end.

> *Then I saw a new heaven and a new earth; for the first heaven and the first earth had passed away, and the sea was no more. I also saw the holy city, the new Jerusalem, coming down out of heaven from God, prepared like a bride adorned for her husband.*
> **REVELATION 21:1-2**

It is the grand finale of miracles because no further miracles will be necessary thereafter. No longer will miraculous healings or miraculous endings to wars be necessary because all diseases and wars will be forever ended. This first miracle of Jesus was at a wedding. His final miracle will be at a wedding as well.

What gave Jesus the right to transform water into anything?

Marriage is a big deal to God. Why did this miracle take place at a wedding?

THE MIRACLES OF CHRIST

LEVELS OF BIBLICAL LEARNING STATEMENT

Jesus, because He is God, had the power to perform miracles, and He did so as a sign of His divine nature and to help people overcome their lack of faith.

Some things just can't be explained. They don't fit inside the neat system we've set up for examining the world. We can predict where a ball will land if we throw it, but we're not very good at explaining the feeling you get in your stomach before something really important happens.

We might completely figure these things out some day. But while Jesus was on Earth, He did some things we'll never be able to crack. He turned water into wine. He walked on top of water. He made a storm go away just by speaking. What's most incredible is that He did all of this for a specific purpose. Today, we're going to look at one miracle He did that you might have overlooked before. What it means will absolutely amaze you.

What miracles have you heard Jesus did? Which is the most amazing to you, and why?

WONDER OF CREATION

Try to think of the most incredible thing you've ever seen. Some people have been lucky enough to go see something amazing on Earth, like the Grand Canyon or Niagara Falls. You might have seen a meteor shower or photos of a distant galaxy from a Space telescope.

When have you seen something that filled you with wonder? What was it?

How would you explain the feeling of wonder to someone who had never experienced it before?

Jesus was something of an expert in wonder. When John was describing Jesus, he said, "All things were created through him, and apart from him not one thing was created that has been created" (John 1:3). Paul elaborated a little bit on this, saying we have "one Lord, Jesus Christ. All things are through him, and we exist through him" (1 Cor. 8:6).

If there is one thing consistent in anything that brings us wonder—whether it's the stars in the sky or the sand on a beach—it's the reason for its existence. We have it because of Jesus Christ. He's really good at making things that blow our minds.

Since everything we see has the same Creator, it all fits in the same set of rules. In fact, God's Universe is so ordered and logical that we can observe something and predict how it will behave in the future. If you drop a rock off of a bridge, you know exactly what will happen to it. If someone observes a comet far off in space, they can predict where it will move. Chairs don't turn into frogs, and items don't pop in and out of existence at random. Through Jesus, we have an extremely logical, ordered Universe.

What do you think of when you hear the word *miracles*?

In your own words, what is a miracle? Have you ever seen one?

Jesus performed a lot of miracles. You may have heard of the time He turned water into wine, or the time He turned a few loaves of bread and a couple of fish into enough food to feed thousands. His miracles all proved a point: He is God. But they did something else: They strengthened the faith of those who witnessed them.

WONDER OF HEALING

Let's take a close look at one of these miracles that Jesus performed to help see this a little more clearly. We will first try to understand why this miracle was such a big deal, and then we will discover something incredible about the One who performed it.

When Luke wrote his account, he paid very close attention to detail to help us "feel" the scene. Read Luke 8:40-48.

Pay attention to verses 42 and 45. What words does Luke include to tell you how chaotic this situation was?

What was happening at the very beginning of this passage? What problem were they dealing with before the sick woman touched Jesus?

Luke went out of his way to show us how hectic the crowd was that day. First of all, they were trying to help a desperate father whose daughter was dying. Second, there was an enormous crowd that was so close together it was "nearly crushing" (v. 42) them.

So when this woman reached out and touched Jesus, there was no way a regular person would've felt anything special. The crowd was so thick that everyone was touching Him! But He knew there was something special about this woman.

Now, your Bible probably says that she had suffered "from bleeding for twelve years" (v. 43). Luke's audience would've known what this meant, but it gets lost a little bit on us. There's actually a passage in the Old Testament that shows us just how extreme her condition was.

Read Leviticus 15:25-28. Note what happens to the things she touches.

When Leviticus tells said someone was "unclean," it doesn't necessarily mean they are sinful—it just means they have to take some extra steps before they can re-enter society. For example, someone who had a skin disease would be considered "unclean" because they could transmit their diseases to other people and spread them. The same goes with someone who is bleeding a lot: Blood carries diseases, so it is important to keep them away from others until they stop bleeding.

WONDER OF SALVATION

The woman mentioned in Luke 8:40-48 had been bleeding for 12 years! This was a serious condition for her—both for her physical health and for her social status.

Together, try to guess what this woman's daily life looked like. What challenges do you think she faced on a daily basis?

How do you think the people around her treated her?

She had probably lived the last twelve years of her life in complete isolation and frustration. She kept going to doctors to get better, but none of them could find a cure for her condition.

[She] had endured much under many doctors. She had spent everything she had and was not helped at all. On the contrary, she became worse.
MARK 5:26

She was broke, broken, and hopeless.

But then she heard about this man people were calling the Son of God. They said He could do amazing things, like walk on top of the water and make diseases going away just by touching those who needed healing.

Re-read Luke 8:44-48. What happened to her after she touched Jesus' robe? How did Jesus react? How does this interaction make you feel?

What do you think Jesus meant when He said, "Your faith has saved you"?

There's no doubt this woman put as much faith as she had in as much of Jesus as she knew. And that was enough to heal her. When Jesus performs a miracle, He does it to strengthen the faith of those who witness it—faith in Him as the one and only Son of God.

BEING // Because Jesus took our sin and gave us His righteousness in its place we are now accepted into God's presence—even though we were once separated from God.

DOING // Because Christianity necessarily involves following Christ, we should continually live in obedience to His commands as an expression of our faith in and love for Him.

APOLOGETIC // Whereas many claim that Jesus was a good man or a great teacher, the truth is that Jesus is God (John 1:1,14; 8:58; 10:30).

CHRIST

Whenever Christ performed a miracle—and whenever anybody in the early church did the same in His name—the purpose was extremely simple: They were making a way for the news of Jesus to be preached. These miracles validated the message that followed. Every time we see a miracle in the Bible, its purpose was to point those who witnessed it back to God.

Jesus may not use you to do supernatural things in His name, but you still have the opportunity to use your actions to make His name known. How can you use your actions to point people to Christ?

COMMUNITY

In Acts 2, one of the more interesting miracles is recorded. There were a bunch of people from all over the world who had made a trip to Jerusalem, which happened to also be the place where the disciples were waiting. Then, all at once, the disciples started preaching the gospel to these people—but the amazing thing was that these people from all over heard what they were saying in their own languages. They knew what was going on in this community of believers was something they needed to be a part of. Before long, at least 3,000 people got saved.

How can we make our Christian communities places people can't wait to be a part of?

CULTURE

Miracles were just one way the gospel message was made accessible to people who didn't believe. For instance, when Paul visited Athens, He didn't have to perform miracles in order to get them to listen to Him; instead, He went to a place where people were holding debates about philosophy and pagan gods. He then used their own debate style and patterns of speech to tell them about Jesus in a way they would have understood (Acts 17:16-34).

What are some ways we can use methods that people understand in order to help them see and understand the gospel message?

Session 4

DEVOTIONS

MIRACULOUS CATCH

After speaking to a large crowd from Simon's boat on Lake Gennesaret, Jesus said to Simon:

> *"Put out into deep water and let down your nets for a catch."*
> *"Master," Simon replied, "we've worked hard all night long and caught nothing. But if you say so, I'll let down the nets." When they did this, they caught a great number of fish, and their nets began to tear. So they signaled to their partners in the other boat to come and help them; they came and filled both boats so full that they began to sink. When Simon Peter saw this, he fell at Jesus's knees and said, "Go away from me, because I'm a sinful man, Lord!" For he and all those with him were amazed at the catch of fish they had taken, and so were James and John, Zebedee's sons, who were Simon's partners. "Don't be afraid," Jesus told Simon. "From now on you will be catching people." Then they brought the boats to land, left everything, and followed him.*
> **LUKE 5:4-11**

Once again, we see that Jesus has come so we may have life in abundance. May the strained fishing nets in this story be a picture of your fruitfulness as someone who shares the gospel.

Why did Simon Peter tell Jesus to go away from him?

Peter would not have gotten very far if he had dragged his net with him on land. What are the nets from your former life you have tried to bring with you as you follow Jesus?

CASTING OUT DEMONS

Demons are real. We need only glimpse at our broken world fraught with terrible acts of evil to see that. However, Christians should not fear demons. Though demons wield fear, they are not themselves immune from it. In fact, did you know that demons are terrified? They are absolutely terrified of Jesus. Most of the biblical narratives describing their speech indicate that, when demons speak, they scream in terror. They cried out (Mark 1:23). They fled to inhabit a herd of pigs and ran the pigs off a cliff (Matt. 8).

Just before the pig incident, look closely at what they asked Jesus:

> *When he had come to the other side, to the region of the Gadarenes, two demon-possessed men met him as they came out of the tombs. They were so violent that no one could pass that way. Suddenly they shouted, "What do you have to do with us, Son of God? Have you come here to torment us before the time?"*
> **MATTHEW 8:28-29**

What is "the time" these demons refer to?

Why were the demons so completely horrified to see Jesus?

Should Christians, filled with the Holy Spirit of God, fear demons? Why, or why not?

HEALING THE LEPER

After another narrative showing Jesus' authority to drive out demons, look to another kind of miracle in Jesus ministry.

> He went into all of Galilee, preaching in their synagogues and driving out demons. Then a man with leprosy came to him and, on his knees, begged him: "If you are willing, you can make me clean." Moved with compassion, Jesus reached out his hand and touched him. "I am willing," he told him. "Be made clean."
> **MARK 1:39-41**

Look closely at this former leper's theology. As you study the Gospel of Mark, you will come upon people unsure of whether or not Jesus was capable of performing a miracle. That is not the case in this story. This man knew Jesus was able to heal him; he wondered only if Jesus was willing to heal him.

Did you notice Jesus touched him? This was significant because lepers were not touched. There are varying degrees of severity in leprosy, but even the mildest case of "scaly" skin (from which the disease is named) would make someone ceremonially unclean and therefore an outcast. It is possible this man had to shout out, "Unclean! Unclean!" as people approached him.

What do you think it was like for this man to be shown compassion by Jesus?

What does this miracle teach us about Jesus' character?

5

THE PRIESTHOOD OF CHRIST

ENGAGE

LEVELS OF BIBLICAL LEARNING STATEMENT

Because no sin can enter God's presence and because Jesus is holy, He is the only way people can connect with God.

We cannot imagine a world without sin. Everywhere we look, sin has caused devastation and heartbreak and violence and injustice. Inside of our hearts, it wreaks havoc. It is easy for us to become bitter, angry, jealous, or filled with impure thoughts.

But that isn't the way it was supposed to be. God made us to live in community with Him: to walk and talk with Him the same way we do with our friends. But we broke that fellowship, and we break it fresh every day. Fortunately, Jesus gave us a way to make it right again.

How would you explain what sin is to someone who had never heard of it before?

SIN BREAKS FELLOWSHIP WITH GOD

What is a food that you just can't stand eating?

We may be fully capable of eating those foods but we don't because we hate them! God has a similar reaction to our sin, though with even more serious consequences. He detests it.

Out loud, read the ways God describes looking at sin:

Why do you want more beatings? Why do you keep on rebelling? The whole head is hurt, and the whole heart is sick. From the sole of the foot even to the head, no spot is uninjured— wounds, welts, and festering sores not cleansed, bandaged, or soothed with oil.
ISAIAH 1:5-6

Why do you force me to look at injustice? Why do you tolerate wrongdoing? Oppression and violence are right in front of me. Strife is ongoing, and conflict escalates.
HABAKKUK 1:3

What are some of the descriptions that you saw showing how God sees and interacts with His people's sin?

Why do you think He hates it so much?

What happens to our relationship with God when we sin?

One of the clearest pictures of what happens between us and God when we sin is in Genesis, when the very first people sinned.

God ordered Adam and Eve to leave the Garden and work the ground to survive (Gen. 3:22-24). They were removed from the place where God's presence was. Once, they could walk and talk with Him, live like family in one house. But then they decided that they knew better than He did. They put their own desires above His. They deliberately disobeyed the command He'd given them. They severed their relationship.

SIN PREVENTS HOLY LIVING

If there's something humans have proven throughout history, it's that they're really great at messing everything up. Which is why Jesus was so remarkable. While He was fully God, He was also fully human—and He was completely perfect.

But we see something that sets Jesus apart very early on in His ministry.

> Just then a man with an unclean spirit was in their synagogue. He cried out, "What do you have to do with us, Jesus of Nazareth? Have you come to destroy us? I know who you are—the Holy One of God!"
> **MARK 1:23-24**

Who did the demon say Jesus is? Why is this surprising, especially considering who said it?

What do you think it means to be holy?

Holiness does not mean purity or perfection; it comes from a word meaning "set apart." Most of us know what it means to be set apart. We might have a fancy set of clothes we reserve for special occasions, a favorite meal we eat only on certain days, or a go-to friend on tough trivia questions. We even celebrate holidays—days set apart for celebrating something special. But what holiness drives at is being set apart for use by God.

What do you think is the difference between someone who is holy and someone who isn't?

Peter helps us understand what holiness looks like when by contrasting holiness with "the desires of your former ignorance" (1 Pet. 1:14). Put simply: Before we knew Christ, we behaved in a certain way, but after we came to know Him, we behaved, thought, and lived a new way.

What do you think are some examples of "desires of your former ignorance," as Peter said? (Think lust, greed, dishonesty.)

SIN IS DEFEATED BY PUTTING ON CHRIST

This is important to note: The things we do are not what make us holy. Plenty of people who don't call Jesus Lord are generous, honest, and act with integrity. Holiness is deeper than that. And it can only come from one person: Jesus, Himself.

> *Let us walk with decency, as in the daytime: not in carousing and drunkenness; not in sexual impurity and promiscuity; not in quarreling and jealousy. But put on the Lord Jesus Christ, and don't make plans to gratify the desires of the flesh.*
> **ROMANS 13:13-14**
>
> *For those of you who were baptized into Christ have been clothed with Christ.*
> **GALATIANS 3:27**

As believers, wrap ourselves with Jesus the way we'd wrap ourselves with a blanket on a cold night. When people see us, we want them to see Jesus, too.

In your own words, what does it mean to "put on" Jesus? What does this look like for you—in your school, in your home, in your friend groups?

How would putting on Christ affect the way we interact with the people around us?

Putting on Christ changes us entirely, because when we do, everything about us becomes different. He makes us new. He makes us holy in God's eyes. If we've put on Christ, then it's not just the world who sees Him; God does, too.

By ourselves we are not holy. We're sinful people in desperate need of a Savior. Our hearts are detestable to God to the point that our sin actually makes Him sick. But Jesus is totally different: He is perfect. He's the only one worthy of standing in the Father's presence. This means He is the only One who can bring us into God's presence—and it can only happen if you are covered by His sacrifice.

When people look at you, what do they see? Do they see you or do they see Jesus?

What is your next step in setting yourself aside and putting on Christ?

> **BEING //** Because Jesus took our sin and gave us His righteousness in its place we are now accepted into God's presence—even though we were once separated from God.
>
> **DOING //** Because Christianity necessarily involves following Christ, we should continually live in obedience to His commands as an expression of our faith in and love for Him.
>
> **APOLOGETIC //** Whereas many claim that Jesus was a good man or a great teacher, the truth is that Jesus is God (John 1:1,14; 8:58; 10:30).

CHRIST

You can tell a lot about someone by the clothes they wear. If you see someone in sweatpants and a comfy t-shirt, you might assume they have an easy day coming up and plan on being home. If you see someone dressed up in a tux, you would probably assume that have a fancy event to attend. In Romans 13:14, Paul told us to "put on...Christ" if we want to avoid gratifying the desires of the flesh. As Christians, we are to "wear" Christ, to put on His attributes and act the way that He would act.

What attributes of Jesus should we be imitating?

Would you say it's difficult or easy to imitate Christ? Explain.

COMMUNITY

When Paul wrote to the Roman church to put on Christ, he wasn't writing to one specific person, but to an entire group of people. A whole church full of believers in Christ would have read the letter he wrote, just as we are reading it today. As individuals we should do as Jesus would have done and we as an entire body of believers should be doing the same. There are some advantages that come with "putting on Christ" as a whole body of people—we all have different things we're good at, areas of influence, and ways we express ourselves. If we leverage our different strengths, we can take steps toward being the body of Christ.

What do you think the advantages are of being a whole body of believers acting like Christ?

CULTURE

There is not a single person on Earth who would be exempt from Jesus' sacrifice. Paul said everyone who calls on the name of the Lord will be saved (Rom. 10:13), no matter who they are or what they look like or where they live. The message of Christ tears down national boundaries, racial divides, and economic gaps and puts us all in the same boat. We are all sinners, and we all have access to the incredible sacrifice Jesus made on our behalf.

How does the gospel put everyone on equal footing?

Who is someone (or a group of people) you think needs to hear the gospel?

Session 5

DEVOTIONS

HEALING THE CENTURION

Jesus' miraculous healing of the Centurion's servant is fascinating because the person being healed was not even physically present (Matt. 8:5-13). In this story, the person healed did not even speak to Jesus. It was not the faith of the afflicted one crying out, but the faith of an advocate speaking on behalf of the one to be healed. Usually, in Jesus' miracles, Jesus was in the direct physical presence of the one He healed. In the story of the Centurion's servant, however, the healed one was some distance away.

> *When he entered Capernaum, a centurion came to him, pleading with him,*
> *"Lord, my servant is lying at home paralyzed, in terrible agony." He said to him,*
> *"Am I to come and heal him?"*
> *"Lord," the centurion replied, "I am not worthy to have you come under my roof.*
> *But just say the word, and my servant will be healed."*
> **MATTHEW 8:5-8**

Jesus marveled that this Roman, likely raised by pagans, had greater faith than all the learned leaders of Israel he had encountered up to that point. He healed the man's servant in the way He would heal someone today. Rather than by direct presence, He healed as an answer to a plea on someone's behalf.

Who has been your centurion? Who has plead with Jesus on your behalf? Pray a prayer of thanks for that person now.

Now, it is your turn to be the centurion. Go before the Lord on someone's behalf and journal that prayer.

HEALING THE MAN BORN BLIND

Why do horrific things befall people who seem to have done nothing to deserve them? Why would our good God allow something unspeakable to happen to a baby, like allowing that baby to be born blind?

> *As he was passing by, he saw a man blind from birth. His disciples asked him: "Rabbi, who sinned, this man or his parents, that he was born blind?"*
> **JOHN 9:1-2**

Jesus' disciples asked a question that is still common in our culture and even popularized by the pagan understanding of "karma," which says the things that happen to us are tied to the things that we do. They assumed someone had to have done something wrong. But Jesus' answer turns that thinking on its head.

> *"Neither this man nor his parents sinned," Jesus answered. "This came about so that God's works might be displayed in him."*
> **JOHN 9:3**

Then, Jesus performed the weirdest miracle ever. He spat on the ground, smeared the mud on the man's face, and told him to go and wash his face in a fountain (John 9:6-7). The parallels to the gospel are striking: Jesus did the work, the filthy was made clean, the blind man was made to see, and the whole thing ended with the saved one being sent. In fact, that is the name of the fountain: "Sent" (John 9:7).

Why do you think Jesus used mud this way?

Why did Jesus say this man was born blind in the first place? How did that differ from the disciples' assumption?

What afflictions in your own life might be used to demonstrate the works of God?

HEALING THE PARALYTIC

Do you have that one friend who just completely lacks discretion? If you cannot think of one, you are likely that crazy friend. The formerly paralyzed man in Mark 2 had several crazy friends. They were so drastic in their measures to get their paralyzed friend to Jesus that they dug a hole through someone's roof to drop him down in front of Jesus. Jesus saw their faith and proclaimed the paralyzed man forgiven. Look at what Mark said about the onlooking critics' reaction:

> But some of the scribes were sitting there, questioning in their hearts: "Why does he speak like this? He's blaspheming! Who can forgive sins but God alone?" Right away Jesus perceived in his spirit that they were thinking like this within themselves and said to them, "Why are you thinking these things in your hearts? Which is easier: to say to the paralytic, 'Your sins are forgiven,' or to say, 'Get up, take your mat, and walk'? But so that you may know that the Son of Man has authority on earth to forgive sins"—he told the paralytic— "I tell you: get up, take your mat, and go home." Immediately he got up, took the mat, and went out in front of everyone. As a result, they were all astounded and gave glory to God, saying, "We have never seen anything like this!"
> **MARK 2:6-12**

Which is the greater miracle here, the healing of a paralyzed man or the proclamation of a sinner forgiven? Why?

These friends did everything they could to get their friend to Jesus. Think about one friend you have who needs to know Jesus. What would you do to get that friend to Jesus? Explain.

6

THE SALVATION OF CHRIST

LEVELS OF BIBLICAL LEARNING STATEMENT

From the beginning, God planned that Jesus would save people from their sins, and it was necessary that He would be crucified and raised.

There's something beautiful about a plan that goes perfectly. Everything is planned for, everything is performed to perfection, and the outcome is exactly the one hoped for. We see it all the time in movies and TV shows, and the result is so satisfying.

God has a plan, too. And since He's God, the plan is perfect. And a little bit mind-blowing. What's more, this plan centers entirely around Jesus. He carried it out—and continues carrying it out—to perfection.

Have you ever had a plan go exactly as you wanted it to? It might have been something simple, like a family vacation. It might have been something bigger, like a surprise birthday party. Tell us about it.

GOD'S PLAN

When some authors sit down to write a story, they don't have anything but a character in mind. They don't know what kinds of things the character will get into until they start putting them in different situations. They might get fired from a job or get a flat tire on the way to school. They might get bitten by a radioactive spider or lose their best friend in a terrible accident. The author puts the character into different situations and sees what kind of story comes out of it.

What is your favorite story? How do you think the author wrote it?

When God writes a story, He doesn't do it in pieces; He has the entire plan in mind at all times. He knows everything that will happen but lets us unravel the mystery one piece at a time. Even when we do things we think surprise Him, He already knew about it.

Even when the things are really bad. When Adam and Eve sinned in the Garden of Eden, He already had a plan in place to fix the relationship we'd broken—and it would involve sacrificing His one and only Son on our behalf.

Before His Son came, God's people looked forward to His coming, and God sprinkled little clues about what He would do throughout their lives. The very first hint came immediately after Adam and Eve sinned. Let's see if we can investigate it and figure out how it shows God's plan.

Read Genesis 3:14-15.

What do you know about what has happened up until this point in the story?

The serpent, which we learned a few weeks ago was the craftiest of all the animals, tempted Eve to directly disobey God's command. So here, God tells the serpent—we could call him the tempter—he would have some trouble with her down the road. Wherever there are people (the woman's offspring), there will be a struggle with the tempter.

But God did more than tell the tempter there would be a struggle between his offspring and the woman's. The tempter may be able to nip at our heels, but what God has to say is far more encouraging for the descendants of Eve (us) than it is for the serpent: Eve's offspring will win.

EARLY CLUES

By connecting snakes with temptation, sin, and death, God was setting His people up for a stunning revelation of just how much He loved them. In fact, the most famous verse in the whole Bible comes because of Israel's history with snakes.

But let's not get ahead of ourselves. We have to see the story as God unfolded it so that we can see how God intended for His Son to conquer sin by dying on the cross, from the beginning.

In Numbers 21, the Israelites found themselves in a bit of a predicament. Like usual, they brought this predicament on themselves. They were wandering around in the wilderness before entering the promised land and, as we've basically come to expect from them, they started complaining. The Israelites were very good at complaining.

Read Numbers 21:4-9.

What are some things you hear people complaining about most often?

Part of the Israelites' problem was that they didn't trust God to provide for them and lead them through the desert. Do you find it easy or difficult to trust God? Why?

When the Israelites started rebelling (again), God sent in poisonous snakes. The Israelites had decided they were more knowledgeable than God was and thought He should do things their way instead of them doing things His way. When God sent in the plague of snakes, they caused all kinds of destruction. People got bitten and died. The consequences of their sin, like the consequences of Adam and Eve's sin, was death.

But God didn't just send death. He also gave them a way to be saved from it. Look at the order of the events. The people sinned. Their sin had a consequence. The people recognized that they were sinful and turned away from it, and then were saved from death through a miracle of God. He didn't take what was hurting them away; instead, He made it so that they could be saved from it by faith.

Why do you think God told them to look at the bronze serpent lifted up on the pole instead of just taking the snakes away?

HOW TO BE FREE

Faith in God to save us from our sins is not something that came in the New Testament. Faith has always been the way God saves His people: more specifically, faith in the One God would send to free us from its consequences forever. The Israelites looked forward to that day—the day Eve's offspring would finally crush the head of the tempter and make His people free.

When that offspring finally arrived, He gave a really interesting explanation about how he'd save people from their sin. He used the same story God had been telling about salvation from the beginning.

> *Read John 3:1-17.*

Here, we're introduced to an interesting character: a really smart, prominent spiritual leader named Nicodemus. He had questions for Jesus about eternal life, but Jesus wanted him to see something different than what he came to find out. He wasn't just going to find out about eternal life, he was going to learn how to be rid of sin's curse.

Which of these verses reminded you of Israel with the snakes? Explain.

How was Jesus' death on the cross like the bronze serpent in Numbers 21?

Many of us have heard John 3:16 before, but when we put it in its context, the verse comes alive. It also connects us with a story God has been telling since the beginning of time: Sin has eternal consequences, but He would send a way for us to be free of those consequences forever. The only way that could happen was for Jesus to be "lifted up" (v. 14).

On your own, take a few minutes to write out your answers to these questions either in a journal or a note on your phone.

What does it mean to believe in something?

Do you believe Jesus saves you from your sin? Why?

LIVE IT OUT

> **BEING //** Because Jesus took our sin and gave us His righteousness in its place we are now accepted into God's presence—even though we were once separated from God.
>
> **DOING //** Because Christianity necessarily involves following Christ, we should continually live in obedience to His commands as an expression of our faith in and love for Him.
>
> **APOLOGETIC //** Whereas many claim that Jesus was a good man or a great teacher, the truth is that Jesus is God (John 1:1,14; 8:58; 10:30).

CHRIST

The most incredible Bible Study that ever happened is recorded for us in Luke 24:13-35. After His resurrection, Jesus found two people walking on the road talking about some of the things that had happened to Jesus in the previous few days. That conversation led up to verse 27, where it says Jesus, "beginning with Moses and all the Prophets, interpreted for them at the things concerning himself in all the Scriptures."

The only Scriptures they had at this time were what we call the Old Testament. Jesus literally had a Bible Study with these two disciples where He started in Genesis ("Moses") and went through the prophets (those smaller books near the end of the Old Testament) to show where He was in all of it. The entire Bible talks about Jesus from cover to cover. It is and always has been about Him.

Look up the following verses. How do you see them talk about Jesus?

- **Genesis 3:15:**

- **Deuteronomy 18:15:**

- **Isaiah 7:14:**

- **Isaiah 9:6:**

COMMUNITY

When Jesus ascended to heaven at the beginning of Acts, He had about 120 followers (Acts 1:15). Though there may have been a few others here and there, the number of people carrying the gospel message was relatively small. Imagine how short the story would have been if those people had kept the message to themselves instead of taking it all over the world!

We have the same opportunity today. We, as the body of Christ, have been entrusted with the message of Jesus, and we're faced with a choice: Do we sit among ourselves and hide it or do we leverage the strength of the group and take it to anybody who needs to hear it? The gospel is one of the only things you guard effectively by giving it away to someone else.

Think about your community of believers, even the ones in this room. How can you all work together to be faithful guardians of the gospel?

CULTURE

You can probably think of people in your own life who don't think much about sin: They pretty much do whatever it is they feel like doing. But we know the truth: Sin is extremely harmful to everyone involved. Even worse, we know sin brings death (Rom. 6:23). But usually, it's not very helpful to walk up to someone and say, "Hey. Stop sinning." Instead, as a Christian, you have an opportunity to live out a life that is actively seeking out sin in your own heart and putting it to death wherever you can. Living this way goes against a culture that tells you, "do whatever you want."

What kind of effect do you think a whole group of people practicing holy living would have on a culture not very concerned with living that way?

How would such a lifestyle stick out?

Session 6

DEVOTIONS

RESURRECTING LAZARUS

Jesus' critics saw Him resurrect a man from the dead. You would think they would immediately see that He is Lord, drop their case against Him, and worship Him. However, they did not. In fact, this miracle set the crucifixion plot in motion.

> *Jesus said to her, "Didn't I tell you that if you believed you would see the glory of God?" So they removed the stone. Then Jesus raised his eyes and said, "Father, I thank you that you heard me. I know that you always hear me, but because of the crowd standing here I said this, so that they may believe you sent me." After he said this, he shouted with a loud voice, "Lazarus, come out!" The dead man came out bound hand and foot with linen strips and with his face wrapped in a cloth. Jesus said to them, "Unwrap him and let him go."*
> **JOHN 11:40-44**

Jesus' prayer was just for the sake of His hearers. Therefore, it was for your sake as John's reader! All of this was to prove Jesus was sent by the Father. So, Jesus' greatest skeptics saw undeniable proof that He is Lord. Rather than worship Him, though, they wanted only to cover up the proof. The same is true of some, but not all, skeptics today.

Summarize Jesus' prayer in this passage.

How does this model the way we should also pray?

THE SPECK AND THE PLANK

Some of Jesus' most profound teachings were given through stories. People who would not believe in Jesus saw them as innocuous little anecdotes. People who believed in Jesus saw them as eternity-altering. The difference between understanding Jesus' parables and not understanding them came down to spiritual ears. If you had the Spirit, then you could understand. If you did not, then you could not. The very first words in this chapter of Matthew are used all the time by people who do not have spiritual ears to hear and so they misuse them:

"Do not judge, so that you won't be judged. For you will be judged by the same standard with which you judge others, and you will be measured by the same measure you use. Why do you look at the splinter in your brother's eye but don't notice the beam of wood in your own eye? Or how can you say to your brother, 'Let me take the splinter out of your eye,' and look, there's a beam of wood in your own eye? Hypocrite! First take the beam of wood out of your eye, and then you will see clearly to take the splinter out of your brother's eye."
MATTHEW 7:1-5

What are some splinters you have noticed in other people's eyes?

What are some wooden beams you have historically not noticed in your own eye? In humble honesty, confess these sins to God now.

THE LOST SHEEP

Here is an often underestimated parable of Jesus'. Frequently, the story of the shepherd leaving behind the ninety-nine to go after the one sheep that went astray is applied to the context of church members who have disappeared for awhile being brought back into fellowship and consistent church attendance. However, look closely at what frames the Parable of the Lost sheep in the context.

> *"See to it that you don't despise one of these little ones, because I tell you that in heaven their angels continually view the face of my Father in heaven. What do you think? If someone has a hundred sheep, and one of them goes astray, won't he leave the ninety-nine on the hillside and go and search for the stray? And if he finds it, truly I tell you, he rejoices over that sheep more than over the ninety-nine that did not go astray. In the same way, it is not the will of your Father in heaven that one of these little ones perish."*
> **MATTHEW 18:10-14**

Remember that all of this was being taught as Jesus held a small boy in His arms (Mark 9:35-37).

This parable shows God's heart toward His children, His heart toward Israel, and His heart toward you. Reading over the quoted Scripture again, what is God's will for His children?

How does God feel about you according to this text?

7

THE PROTECTION OF CHRIST

ENGAGE

LEVELS OF BIBLICAL LEARNING STATEMENT

Jesus sits at God's right hand and continually intercedes for believers as our advocate, mediator, and high priest.

As we have seen, Jesus has always existed within the Godhead as the second person of the Trinity. After His crucifixion and resurrection, Jesus ascended into heaven and the Holy Spirit was sent to dwell within God's people. Jesus is now at the Father's right hand, making intercession for us as we seek to live our lives for His glory.

What does it mean to be an advocate for someone? A mediator?

REMEMBER THE BLOOD

Memories are pretty crazy if you think about it. They're kind of like replaying a movie in your brain, but it's a movie you've lived. Funny enough, one of the best ways to remember something is through smell.

Smell is ridiculously powerful. Your smell receptors are connected to your brain's emotional center, which is why sometimes you smell something and it brings up a powerful memory of another time you smelled that same thing.[1]

What are some of your favorite smells? Why?

Are there any smells that bring up memories for you? What are they?

We use all kinds of senses to remember things, and the Israelites weren't any different. But for them, there was something they were around a lot that brought up bad memories. The sight, smell, and sticky humidity of blood was pretty regular in Israel's society, and it reminded them how sinful they were. Look at how the author of Hebrews says it:

According to the law almost everything is purified with blood, and without the shedding of blood there is no forgiveness.
HEBREWS 9:22

Blood can be pretty gross to think about. When someone says the word *blood*, what comes to mind?

Why do you think some people get a little squeamish when we start talking about blood?

It's a good thing talking about blood makes us feel a little icky. It's almost never a good sign when someone is bleeding. It does all kinds of good things inside of our bodies, but causes some issues when it is on the outside. If you lose too much of it, you can't even survive!

THE NEED FOR ATONEMENT

For hundreds of years, Israel's streets were flowing with blood—the blood of animals. Daily at the temple, people were taking lambs, doves, oxen, and goats to be slaughtered and offered as payment for their sins. The system God set up made sure the people always remembered how serious their sin was, because the smell of blood in the air would never let them forgot.

Even though sacrifice was a regular thing for the Israelites, there was one day that was more important than the rest: the Day of Atonement. And there was one person on the Day of Atonement who was more important than the others: the High Priest. Leviticus 16 tells us all about the Day of Atonement.

> **Read Leviticus 16:3-5,11-16,20-22,27-28,30.**

> **Based on what you read, what do you think it means to atone for something?**

> **When is a time you've had to atone for something you've done?**

Atonement means making amends for something you've done wrong. It's way more than just saying you're sorry; it requires humbling yourself, removing the selfishness that makes you say, "it's not my fault," and going out of your way to make up for the wrong you did.

But the way God feels about sin is obvious because of the brutal way it can be atoned. The penalty for sin, for betraying God's standard, is death.

> **A lot of those Leviticus passages were pretty difficult to read. Imagine how much more difficult they were to perform! How does the sacrificial system help you understand how seriously God takes sin?**

> **How seriously do we take sin today? What makes you think that?**

JESUS IS OUR HIGH PRIEST

It was the High Priest's job, one day a year, to do something nobody else was allowed (or able) to do: enter God's holy place and atone for the sins God's people committed. Year after year, decade after decade, century after century, this was one of the High Priest's most important tasks. But it never stopped, because animal sacrifices made by sinful humans were only temporary. There was no lamb spotless enough to cover sin once and for all, and no priest holy enough to offer such a sacrifice.

> *Now many have become Levitical priests, since they are prevented by death from remaining in office. But because he remains forever, he holds his priesthood permanently. Therefore, he is able to save completely those who come to God through him, since he always lives to intercede for them.*
> **HEBREWS 7:23-25.**

Once, people had to provide their own sacrifices for the priest to offer. But then Jesus came along as our new High Priest and gave the only sacrifice that could cover all sin forever: Himself. But this passage also says He does something else for us. It's a fancy word called *intercession*.

Without looking it up, do you know what intercession is? When might you have someone intercede for you?

If someone intercedes for you, that means they step in on your behalf and take your side. We might think of lawyers as people who intercede for us: they argue our case in front of a judge so that we don't have to.

> *Who is the one who condemns? Christ Jesus is the one who died, but even more, has been raised; he also is at the right hand of God and intercedes for us.*
> **ROMANS 8:34**

How awesome is that picture! Even though we are not perfect by any means, if we've put ourselves under Jesus' authority, He is standing before God right this second arguing for us. And because Jesus is constantly interceding for those who are His children, we are His forever.

As you close your study time together, take some time alone with Jesus. Read back over some of the passages we've explored and thank Jesus for what they tell you He's done for you.

> **BEING //** Because Jesus took our sin and gave us His righteousness in its place we are now accepted into God's presence—even though we were once separated from God.
>
> **DOING //** Because Christianity necessarily involves following Christ, we should continually live in obedience to His commands as an expression of our faith in and love for Him.
>
> **APOLOGETIC //** Whereas many claim that Jesus was a good man or a great teacher, the truth is that Jesus is God (John 1:1,14; 8:58; 10:30).

CHRIST

A man named John was in court because he was accused of stealing property from the people he was staying with. When his name came up on the judge's list, the judge called it out for the whole court to hear: "Is John present?" But John didn't have to say anything at all. Instead, his attorney stood and said, "He's present, your honor." The attorney stepped in and had the judge look at him instead of at John—the judge would be dealing with the attorney from that point on.

That's what Jesus does for us as our advocate. When God looks at you and says, "what right do you have to come into my presence," Jesus stands in your defense and says, "He's with me. I've already covered him."

How does knowing what Christ did and is doing for you affect the way you see yourself?

COMMUNITY

We have to be careful not to be trapped in a "me only" gospel. Everybody who has been saved by Christ is in the same situation: None of us deserves it, but we all received His grace anyway. He's not only interceding for you, He's interceding for everyone who is called by His name. This is a truth that should bind us together and unite us under the same banner: the grace of our Savior, Jesus.

Do you feel connected with the people in your church?

How do you think we can make biblical community a place people feel more welcomed and connected?

CULTURE

It is comforting to know Jesus is actively fighting for us. It feels good to know someone is in your corner. Because we know what that feels like, we have an opportunity to show that to other people, also. There are people all around us who need someone to fight for them, or at the very least stand with them and let them know they are not alone.

Who are people today who may not know Jesus, but need to know that someone is there for them? How can you be someone who is there for them?

How do you think standing with them could help them see Jesus?

Session 7

DEVOTIONS

THE TENANT FARMERS

Toward the end of His ministry, Jesus stopped being so covert. He no longer shushed people after healing them. He no longer miraculously disappeared through crowds as they tried to kill Him because it was not yet His time. Instead, He began to teach parables that were more "in-your-face" to the Pharisees. In Matthew 21:33-46, He told them a parable about a farmer who leased His vineyard to some tenant farmers who abused, killed, and stoned his messengers. These symbolized the martyred prophets of the Old Testament. The farm owner in Jesus' parable then sent his son.

> *"But when the tenant farmers saw the son, they said to each other, 'This is the heir. Come, let's kill him and take his inheritance.' So they seized him, threw him out of the vineyard, and killed him. Therefore, when the owner of the vineyard comes, what will he do to those farmers?"*
> **MATTHEW 21:38-40**

Then, stepping right into it and proving their guilt, the Pharisees responded:

> *"He will completely destroy those terrible men," they told him, "and lease his vineyard to other farmers who will give him his fruit at the harvest."*
> **MATTHEW 21:41**

At long last, Jesus revealed to the Pharisees that He had been speaking about them in this parable. Likely, this was also the moment they realized they had been the bad guys in His parables several times over the previous three years.

At what point in this parable did Jesus reveal that He knew His death was coming.

Do you believe the Pharisees inadvertently admitted their guilt by doing exactly what Jesus said they would do in this parable? Why or why not?

THE SOWER

Two missionaries, both equally equipped, can go to different countries on mission and come back with a huge disparity between their stories. One may have led hundreds to Christ while the other comes back having led only one or two. Why? This is because people's hearts are different. The two missionaries were sharing the same gospel, but one was casting the seeds of the gospel onto hard hearts while the other was sharing the gospel with people spiritually ready to receive it.

> *"Listen! Consider the sower who went out to sow. As he sowed, some seed fell along the path, and the birds came and devoured it. Other seed fell on rocky ground where it didn't have much soil, and it grew up quickly, since the soil wasn't deep. When the sun came up, it was scorched, and since it had no root, it withered away. Other seed fell among thorns, and the thorns came up and choked it, and it didn't produce fruit. Still other seed fell on good ground and it grew up, producing fruit that increased thirty, sixty, and a hundred times."*
> **MARK 4:3-8**

In the subsequent verses, Jesus explained that the bird represents Satan, the rocky soil represents the false conversion of a shallow Christian, the thorns represent wealth and the things of this world, and the good soil represents the Christian who disciples others into evangelism.

Explain why the Holy Spirit is able to till the hardened soil of other people's hearts while you are not able to.

Are you honestly prepared for the scorching sun to come out and test your faith? Are there thorns growing in your life that you need to invite God to rip up? If so, confess them here.

THE LOST COIN

Jesus' Parable of the Lost Coin gives us insight as to how heaven feels about a sinner repenting. Hint: it is basically a massive party.

> *"Or what woman who has ten silver coins, if she loses one coin, does not light a lamp, sweep the house, and search carefully until she finds it? When she finds it, she calls her friends and neighbors together, saying, 'Rejoice with me, because I have found the silver coin I lost!' I tell you, in the same way, there is joy in the presence of God's angels over one sinner who repents."*
> **LUKE 15:8-10**

God is about the business of pursuing the hearts of those who will believe. Draw upon the imagery Jesus gave in this parable and imagine what it is like in heaven when you are sharing the gospel with someone. The celebration that breaks out among the angels is greater in volume and eternally greater in significance than a championship-game-winning touchdown celebration. Consider the number of Christians out there in the world sharing their faith right this moment. From heaven's perspective of time, it must be phenomenal and frequent.

With whom could you share the gospel and offer a chance to repent today?

When he or she does repent, what will happen in heaven? Which Bible passage gives you your answer?

Did heaven break into celebration when you repented? What does this reveal about God's heart toward you?

ENGAGE

The stadium is full. All of the opening acts have finished, and you are just moments away from your favorite band taking the stage. You've been waiting for it for what seems like forever, and now it's so close to being here that you can almost taste it. Your heart starts beating faster, you're shuffling around with nervous excitement for the moment the lights go out and you know the show is about to begin.

There are few things more exciting than the moments just before something we've been waiting for gets started. We know it'll come; all we have to do is wait for it. Just before Jesus left after His resurrection, He made a promise: He's coming back. And when He does, absolutely everything will change.

When have you experienced the nervous excitement of waiting for something to start?

THE END IN SIGHT

When all of a story's conflicts have finished, all of the characters have made their final decisions, and the loose threads are tied up neatly, the ending can happen. Otherwise, it's not a very satisfying story at all. There's a word for the final moments of the story: the denouement.

The story God has been telling since the beginning of creation has many of the same things the stories you just talked about have. It has a great number of conflicts, a vast enemy, and, most importantly, an ending already in mind. In fact, Scripture tells us how the story will end, and it will end with victory.

When most of us think about telling the end of the story, we immediately think of the Book of Revelation. But that is far from the first time we hear about how God will end His story. And every single time we hear about it, the ending is always the same; it ends with Jesus on the throne.

Out loud, read some of the Old Testament passages that talk about Jesus reigning on the throne, and answer the following question about them:

How do you think these passages reference Jesus coming to reign?

- **Isaiah 9:6-7:**

- **Jeremiah 23:5:**

- **Daniel 7:13-14:**

- **Psalm 22:27-31:**

There are dozens of places in the Old Testament that talk about the Messiah coming to rule over creation and make all things new, but New Testament writers knew the exact same thing was true.

What do each of them say about what He will do?

- **Luke 1:26-33:**

- **Acts 3:17-21:**

- **2 Thessalonians 1:6-7:**

THE RETURN OF THE KING

Here's the picture of what has happened by the time we get to the passage we're about to read. Jesus has been betrayed by one of His closest friends, questioned in multiple courts, mocked and spat on by a crowd of people, flogged to within an inch of His life, nailed through the wrists and feet to a wooden plank, and left to die. But even more, Jesus became the perfect sacrificial lamb, bearing the sins of the entire world. He's withstanding not only indescribable pain and humiliation, but was also feeling the weight of the sins of anybody who would ever believe in Him. That's when this happens:

> *From noon until three in the afternoon darkness came over the whole land.*
> *About three in the afternoon Jesus cried out with a loud voice, "Elí, Elí, lemá*
> *sabachtháni?" that is, "My God, my God, why have you abandoned me?"*
> **MATTHEW 27:45-46**

Some thought He was calling for Elijah. Some thought He'd gone crazy. But those who knew Him as a Rabbi would've known something else: He was teaching them a lesson explaining what had happened and what was going to happen next. What Jesus was telling those listening to what He was actually saying was, "Turn with me to Psalm 22."

Read Psalm 22.

What parts of this Psalm remind you of what was currently happening to Jesus?

Describe in your own words how the Psalm ends.

Why do you think Jesus wanted His followers to hear this?

Even in the darkest hour of His life, Jesus was telling His disciples it wasn't over. He was being crushed like a worm for our sins, but Kingship still belongs to Him. The grave wouldn't keep Him, and when He returned He'd be bringing all of heaven with Him.

ALL THINGS NEW

We live in an extremely fortunate time. We don't have to sacrifice goats or lambs or pigeons to atone for our sins. We get to hold copies of the Bible in our hands. We can read the whole of God's story all at once, and see the big picture of what God has done, what He is doing, and what He will do in time to come. Best of all, we know that He will make things new.

When John saw a prophecy of things to come, this is how he wrote it would be once Jesus came back.

> Then I heard a loud voice from the throne: Look, God's dwelling is with humanity, and he will live with them. They will be his peoples, and God himself will be with them and will be their God. He will wipe away every tear from their eyes. Death will be no more; grief, crying, and pain will be no more, because the previous things have passed away.
> **REVELATION 21:3–4**

The only thing we have to do to inherit the life God promises us is submit to the lordship of His Son: the perfect, sinless Son of God who was killed on our behalf, who was raised from the dead, who returned to heaven, and who will come again.

As you close your time together, take a few minutes to get alone with God and answer these questions:

Jesus will come again to rule over creation. But does He rule your heart now? If not, why not?

You've learned a lot about Jesus over the course of these few weeks. What is your next step?

Who is one person you know who needs to hear about Jesus?

BEING // Because Jesus took our sin and gave us His righteousness in its place we are now accepted into God's presence—even though we were once separated from God.

DOING // Because Christianity necessarily involves following Christ, we should continually live in obedience to His commands as an expression of our faith in and love for Him.

APOLOGETIC // Whereas many claim that Jesus was a good man or a great teacher, the truth is that Jesus is God (John 1:1,14; 8:58; 10:30).

CHRIST

Jesus is sovereign. He is in control of everything, meaning there is nothing you could ever experience that He doesn't know about—even the really difficult things. Not one person will get through life without knowing hard times, but those of us who know Jesus can endure them with hope. Our hope is that Jesus is risen, reigning, and promises to make all things new.

How do you think difficulties and tough times help us see Jesus?

What is something you're going through right now that can draw you closer to Christ?

COMMUNITY

God's kingdom doesn't just refer to the kingdom He will come back to set up; it's something He said was here, now. He said we don't just point to a place and say, "Look there's God's kingdom!" He said, "You see, the kingdom of God is in your midst" (Luke 17:21). Just as you are still a citizen of the United States even if you're in a foreign country, we are members of God's kingdom even though we're living on this temporary Earth. We are His kingdom because we are His people, and we will populate it when He comes back to rule.

What does it mean to you to be a citizen of the United States? How does that help you see what it means to be a part of the kingdom of God?

CULTURE

As Christians, we eagerly await the day Jesus comes back to take His church home. But that doesn't mean we're sitting on our hands, looking at the sky, and praying the day comes soon. Jesus will come to rule over His kingdom on earth, but we can also go before Him and bring His kingdom to people here, today. There is an entire world who doesn't know who Jesus is and doesn't know the joy of living in His kingdom, and we have the opportunity to show them what that is like.

How can you bring the kingdom of God to people who aren't part of it?

Session 8

DEVOTIONS

THE PHARISEE AND THE TAX COLLECTOR

We tend to trust in our own righteousness to save ourselves. This is the height of arrogance and— if we let this thinking permeate our minds—it contorts our view of ourselves to cause us to look down on those without Christ as though they just are not as righteous as we are. This was the thinking of the Pharisees and Jesus called them out on that with this parable:

> *"Two men went up to the temple to pray, one a Pharisee and the other a tax collector. The Pharisee was standing and praying like this about himself: 'God, I thank you that I'm not like other people—greedy, unrighteous, adulterers, or even like this tax collector. I fast twice a week; I give a tenth of everything I get.'*
> *"But the tax collector, standing far off, would not even raise his eyes to heaven but kept striking his chest and saying, 'God, have mercy on me, a sinner!' I tell you, this one went down to his house justified rather than the other; because everyone who exalts himself will be humbled, but the one who humbles himself will be exalted."*
> **LUKE 18:10-14**

The Pharisee was the most respected religious leader in town. The tax collector, the most despised. However, the tax collector demonstrated brokenness over his sin and so was justified freely by the grace of God. That we sinners, though guilty, may be found justified before our holy God is nothing short of grace.

Have you been parading your righteousness before others on social media? If so, when?

As the grace of God is poured out on this tax collector after such a contrite confession, how do you think he felt?

THE WEEDS AND THE WHEAT

Have you observed "fake Christianity"? Have you been guilty of it in the past? Jesus shared how God feels about it and even gave a parable that shows what will become of those who claim to know Jesus, but are actually far from Him. In Matthew 13:24-30, Jesus gave the parable of a man who sowed good seed in his field, but was sabotaged when an enemy came behind him to plant the seeds of weeds. The farm hands asked if they should pull of the weeds, but the farmer told them to let both grow until the harvest where they will burn up the bundles of weeds and bring the wheat into the barn.

Jesus gave an interpretation of this parable a few verses later, explaining:

> He replied: "The one who sows the good seed is the Son of Man; the field is the world; and the good seed—these are the children of the kingdom. The weeds are the children of the evil one, and the enemy who sowed them is the devil. The harvest is the end of the age, and the harvesters are angels. Therefore, just as the weeds are gathered and burned in the fire, so it will be at the end of the age."
> **MATTHEW 13:37-40**

Hell is an unpopular teaching, but fake Christianity is a popular practice. What is the connection there?

Does disliking this teaching make it less true? Why or why not?

Based on this text, can we expect God to uproot fake Christians, or let them continue among the true believers in God's church?

THE TREASURE IN THE FIELD

Every time we forsake God for something else, we get ripped off. Every time we turn away from God, whatever we turn to is less worthy than He. Of all the causes we can invest our single-chance lives in, none is greater than the gospel of Jesus Christ. Listen to one more parable from Jesus:

> *"The kingdom of heaven is like treasure, buried in a field, that a man found and reburied. Then in his joy he goes and sells everything he has and buys that field. "Again, the kingdom of heaven is like a merchant in search of fine pearls. When he found one priceless pearl, he went and sold everything he had and bought it."*
> **MATTHEW 13:44-46**

God and His coming heavenly kingdom are worth every conceivable sacrifice we could make on this earth. Every financial sacrifice we make for the gospel and every personal hardship we endure on its behalf amount ultimately to nothing when compared to what we gain through the gospel. The next time you feel like you have been ripped off in life, just remember you were once a sinner bound toward hell, but are now a Christian bound toward heaven. This is the greatest news of all-time!

What priority have you allowed to creep up your priorities list and even overtake the kingdom of God in your heart?

Journal here a vision for your future that reflects a proper understanding of this passage.

ENGAGE

Start the session by reading the *Levels of Biblical Learning Statement* on page 6. Then, use the introduction provided as a way to begin your group time before transitioning to the Discuss section.

DISCUSS

Be sure to read the Discuss section on pages 7-9 before coming together as a group. Doing so will allow you to be familiar with the material and will help you select which portions of the material you would like to cover in the allotted amount of group time. Look for places in the Discuss section where you can add a personal anecdote to a question or a Scripture passage to share in addition to what has been provided. Making preparations like these will help your group time run more smoothly and be more effective in the end.

LIVE IT OUT

After your group works through the Discuss section, take some time to move through the application found in the Live It Out section on pages 10-11. Look for specific, personal ways you can connect with the material from your own past. Sharing a personal story or illustration that connects with the lesson is a great way to connect with students and creates an atmosphere where students also feel comfortable sharing.

WEEKLY LEADER TIPS

- Introduce the personal devotions that follow Session 1, and remind students to complete the session devotions on pages 12-15 before your next meeting.
- Challenge students to memorize the Levels of Biblical Learning Statement for Session 1.
- Encourage students to be in the habit of building into their personal prayer lives with what they have learned this week.

WEEKLY LEADER NOTES

....

....

....

....

ENGAGE

Start the session by reading the *Levels of Biblical Learning Statement* on page 16. Then, use the introduction provided as a way to begin your group time before transitioning to the Discuss section.

DISCUSS

Be sure to read the Discuss section on pages 17-19 before coming together as a group. Doing so will allow you to be familiar with the material and will help you select which portions of the material you would like to cover in the allotted amount of group time. Look for places in the Discuss section where you can add a personal anecdote to a question or a Scripture passage to share in addition to what has been provided. Making preparations like these will help your group time run more smoothly and be more effective in the end.

LIVE IT OUT

After your group works through the Discuss section, take some time to move through the application found in the Live It Out section on pages 20-21. Look for specific, personal ways you can connect with the material from your own past. Sharing a personal story or illustration that connects with the lesson is a great way to connect with students and creates an atmosphere where students also feel comfortable sharing.

WEEKLY LEADER TIPS

- Introduce the personal devotions that follow Session 2, and remind students to complete the session devotions on pages 22-25 before your next meeting.
- Challenge students to memorize the Levels of Biblical Learning Statement for Session 2.
- Encourage students to be in the habit of building into their personal prayer lives with what they have learned this week.

WEEKLY LEADER NOTES

....

....

....

....

ENGAGE

Start the session by reading the *Levels of Biblical Learning Statement* on page 26. Then, use the introduction provided as a way to begin your group time before transitioning to the Discuss section.

DISCUSS

Be sure to read the Discuss section on pages 27-29 before coming together as a group. Doing so will allow you to be familiar with the material and will help you select which portions of the material you would like to cover in the allotted amount of group time. Look for places in the Discuss section where you can add a personal anecdote to a question or a Scripture passage to share in addition to what has been provided. Making preparations like these will help your group time run more smoothly and be more effective in the end.

LIVE IT OUT

After your group works through the Discuss section, take some time to move through the application found in the Live It Out section on pages 30-31. Look for specific, personal ways you can connect with the material from your own past. Sharing a personal story or illustration that connects with the lesson is a great way to connect with students and creates an atmosphere where students also feel comfortable sharing.

WEEKLY LEADER TIPS

- Introduce the personal devotions that follow Session 3, and remind students to complete the session devotions on pages 32-35 before your next meeting.
- Challenge students to memorize the Levels of Biblical Learning Statement for Session 3.
- Encourage students to be in the habit of building into their personal prayer lives with what they have learned this week.

WEEKLY LEADER NOTES

....

....

....

....

ENGAGE

Start the session by reading the *Levels of Biblical Learning Statement* on page 36. Then, use the introduction provided as a way to begin your group time before transitioning to the Discuss section.

DISCUSS

Be sure to read the Discuss section on pages 37-39 before coming together as a group. Doing so will allow you to be familiar with the material and will help you select which portions of the material you would like to cover in the allotted amount of group time. Look for places in the Discuss section where you can add a personal anecdote to a question or a Scripture passage to share in addition to what has been provided. Making preparations like these will help your group time run more smoothly and be more effective in the end.

LIVE IT OUT

After your group works through the Discuss section, take some time to move through the application found in the Live It Out section on pages 40-41. Look for specific, personal ways you can connect with the material from your own past. Sharing a personal story or illustration that connects with the lesson is a great way to connect with students and creates an atmosphere where students also feel comfortable sharing.

WEEKLY LEADER TIPS

- Introduce the personal devotions that follow Session 4, and remind students to complete the session devotions on pages 42-45 before your next meeting.
- Challenge students to memorize the Levels of Biblical Learning Statement for Session 4.
- Encourage students to be in the habit of building into their personal prayer lives with what they have learned this week.

WEEKLY LEADER NOTES

....

....

....

....

ENGAGE

Start the session by reading the *Levels of Biblical Learning Statement* on page 46. Then, use the introduction provided as a way to begin your group time before transitioning to the Discuss section.

DISCUSS

Be sure to read the Discuss section on pages 47-49 before coming together as a group. Doing so will allow you to be familiar with the material and will help you select which portions of the material you would like to cover in the allotted amount of group time. Look for places in the Discuss section where you can add a personal anecdote to a question or a Scripture passage to share in addition to what has been provided. Making preparations like these will help your group time run more smoothly and be more effective in the end.

LIVE IT OUT

After your group works through the Discuss section, take some time to move through the application found in the Live It Out section on pages 50-51. Look for specific, personal ways you can connect with the material from your own past. Sharing a personal story or illustration that connects with the lesson is a great way to connect with students and creates an atmosphere where students also feel comfortable sharing.

WEEKLY LEADER TIPS

- Introduce the personal devotions that follow Session 5, and remind students to complete the session devotions on pages 52-55 before your next meeting.
- Challenge students to memorize the Levels of Biblical Learning Statement for Session 5.
- Encourage students to be in the habit of building into their personal prayer lives with what they have learned this week.

WEEKLY LEADER NOTES

....

....

....

....

ENGAGE

Start the session by reading the *Levels of Biblical Learning Statement* on page 56. Then, use the introduction provided as a way to begin your group time before transitioning to the Discuss section.

DISCUSS

Be sure to read the Discuss section on pages 57-59 before coming together as a group. Doing so will allow you to be familiar with the material and will help you select which portions of the material you would like to cover in the allotted amount of group time. Look for places in the Discuss section where you can add a personal anecdote to a question or a Scripture passage to share in addition to what has been provided. Making preparations like these will help your group time run more smoothly and be more effective in the end.

LIVE IT OUT

After your group works through the Discuss section, take some time to move through the application found in the Live It Out section on pages 60-61. Look for specific, personal ways you can connect with the material from your own past. Sharing a personal story or illustration that connects with the lesson is a great way to connect with students and creates an atmosphere where students also feel comfortable sharing.

WEEKLY LEADER TIPS

- Introduce the personal devotions that follow Session 6, and remind students to complete the session devotions on pages 62-65 before your next meeting.
- Challenge students to memorize the Levels of Biblical Learning Statement for Session 6.
- Encourage students to be in the habit of building into their personal prayer lives with what they have learned this week.

WEEKLY LEADER NOTES

....

....

....

....

ENGAGE

Start the session by reading the *Levels of Biblical Learning Statement* on page 66. Then, use the introduction provided as a way to begin your group time before transitioning to the Discuss section.

DISCUSS

Be sure to read the Discuss section on pages 67-69 before coming together as a group. Doing so will allow you to be familiar with the material and will help you select which portions of the material you would like to cover in the allotted amount of group time. Look for places in the Discuss section where you can add a personal anecdote to a question or a Scripture passage to share in addition to what has been provided. Making preparations like these will help your group time run more smoothly and be more effective in the end.

LIVE IT OUT

After your group works through the Discuss section, take some time to move through the application found in the Live It Out section on pages 70-71. Look for specific, personal ways you can connect with the material from your own past. Sharing a personal story or illustration that connects with the lesson is a great way to connect with students and creates an atmosphere where students also feel comfortable sharing.

WEEKLY LEADER TIPS

- Introduce the personal devotions that follow Session 7, and remind students to complete the session devotions on pages 72-75 before your next meeting.
- Challenge students to memorize the Levels of Biblical Learning Statement for Session 7.
- Encourage students to be in the habit of building into their personal prayer lives with what they have learned this week.

WEEKLY LEADER NOTES

....

....

....

....

ENGAGE

Start the session by reading the *Levels of Biblical Learning Statement* on page 76. Then, use the introduction provided as a way to begin your group time before transitioning to the Discuss section.

DISCUSS

Be sure to read the Discuss section on pages 77-79 before coming together as a group. Doing so will allow you to be familiar with the material and will help you select which portions of the material you would like to cover in the allotted amount of group time. Look for places in the Discuss section where you can add a personal anecdote to a question or a Scripture passage to share in addition to what has been provided. Making preparations like these will help your group time run more smoothly and be more effective in the end.

LIVE IT OUT

After your group works through the Discuss section, take some time to move through the application found in the Live It Out section on pages 80-81. Look for specific, personal ways you can connect with the material from your own past. Sharing a personal story or illustration that connects with the lesson is a great way to connect with students and creates an atmosphere where students also feel comfortable sharing.

WEEKLY LEADER TIPS

- Introduce the personal devotions that follow Session 8, and remind students to complete the session devotions on pages 82-85 before your next meeting.
- Challenge students to memorize the Levels of Biblical Learning Statement for Session 8.
- Encourage students to be in the habit of building into their personal prayer lives with what they have learned this week.

WEEKLY LEADER NOTES

....

....

....

....

SOURCES

SESSION 2

1. Laura Dean, "ACHOO Syndrome," *National Center for Biotechnology Information*, July 27, 2015, https://www.ncbi.nlm.nih.gov.

SESSION 3

1. Jeff Hale, "A Ghostly Success in a Most Unlikely Place," *American Orchid Society*, accessed April 16, 2019, http://www.aos.org/orchids/additional-resources/a-ghostly-success-in-a-most-unlikely-place.aspx.

2. Rick Warren, *The Purpose Driven Life: What on Earth Am I Here for?* (Grand Rapids, MI: Zondervan, 2012), 149.

SESSION 7

1. "Psychology and Smell," *Fifth Sense*, accessed April 16, 2019, http://www.fifthsense.org.uk/psychology-and-smell/.

STUDY ALL 10 CONCEPTS IN ONE YEAR!

VOL. 1
GOD
005816978

VOL. 2
JESUS
005816979

VOL. 3
HOLY SPIRIT & BIBLE
005816980

VOL. 4
CREATION & PEOPLE
005816982

VOL. 5
SALVATION & CHURCH
005816983

VOL. 6
FAMILY, COMMUNITY & WORLD
005816984

Based on *LifeWay's Levels of Biblical Learning*™, Milestones provides an age-appropriate, systematic approach to leading students through 10 core biblical concepts—God, Jesus, Holy Spirit, Bible, Creation, People, Salvation, Church, Faith, Community and World.

ORDER YOUR NEXT VOLUME AT
LIFEWAY.COM/MILESTONES OR 800.458.2772